My First NFL Book

# DALLAS
# COWBOYS

Nate Cohn

**LET'S READ**
**AV²**
**BY WEIGL™**
**ADDED VALUE • AUDIO VISUAL**

Go to **www.av2books.com**, and enter this book's unique code.

## BOOK CODE

**D 3 2 2 4 5 8**

**AV² by Weigl** brings you media enhanced books that support active learning.

736 1369

AV² provides enriched content that supplements and complements this book. Weigl's AV² books strive to create inspired learning and engage young minds in a total learning experience.

# Your AV² Media Enhanced books come alive with...

**Audio**
Listen to sections of the book read aloud.

**Video**
Watch informative video clips.

**Embedded Weblinks**
Gain additional information for research.

**Try This!**
Complete activities and hands-on experiments.

**Key Words**
Study vocabulary, and complete a matching word activity.

**Quizzes**
Test your knowledge.

**Slide Show**
View images and captions, and prepare a presentation.

# ... and much, much more!

Published by AV² by Weigl
350 5th Avenue, 59th Floor
New York, NY 10118

Website: www.av2books.com

Printed in the United States of America in Brainerd, Minnesota
1 2 3 4 5 6 7 8 9 0  21 20 19 18 17

032017
020317

Editor: Katie Gillespie
Art Director: Terry Paulhus

Weigl acknowledges Getty Images and iStock as the primary image suppliers for this title.

Library of Congress Control Number: 2017930542

ISBN 978-1-4896-5499-1 (hardcover)
ISBN 978-1-4896-5501-1 (multi-user eBook)

My First NFL Book

# DALLAS COWBOYS

## CONTENTS

# Team History

The Dallas Cowboys played their first NFL season in 1960. The team had 20 winning seasons in a row from 1966 to 1985. Coach Tom Landry led the Cowboys during this record number of wins. No one has beaten his streak for winning seasons.

Bob Lilly was the Cowboys' first ever draft pick in 1961.

# The Stadium

The Cowboys play at AT&T Stadium. This is the second-largest building of its kind in the world. The stadium's roof can be opened when the weather is warm. There is a huge TV above the field so fans can see the action up close.

AT&T Stadium is in Arlington, Texas. This is a 30-minute drive from Dallas.

# Team Spirit

Sports reporters sometimes call the Cowboys "America's team." The name comes from a film about the team's fans. The Cowboys' mascot is named Rowdy. He wears a big cowboy hat and boots to show that he is a Cowboys fan. Rowdy often dances on the sidelines.

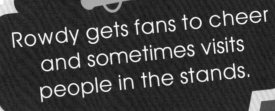

Rowdy gets fans to cheer and sometimes visits people in the stands.

# The Jerseys

The Cowboys' colors are navy blue, silver, and white. The players wear jerseys with stripes on their sleeves for most games. They wear jerseys with a star on the shoulders for special games. The Cowboys sometimes wear different shades of blue as well.

# The Helmet

The Cowboys' helmet is easy to pick out. It is silver with blue and white stripes in the middle. There is a star on each side. The first Cowboys helmets were white. The helmets changed to silver in 1964.

The Cowboys wear the old white helmets for special games.

# The Coach

Jason Garrett is the head coach of the Cowboys. He is the first former Cowboys player to become their head coach. Garrett was part of three winning Super Bowl teams as a Cowboys player. He comes from a Cowboys family. His dad was a scout for the team for 21 years.

# Player Positions

The running back is part of the offense. A player in this position mainly runs with the ball. Some running backs play in the halfback position. This means they are behind the quarterback when the ball snaps into play. Halfbacks can also be called tailbacks.

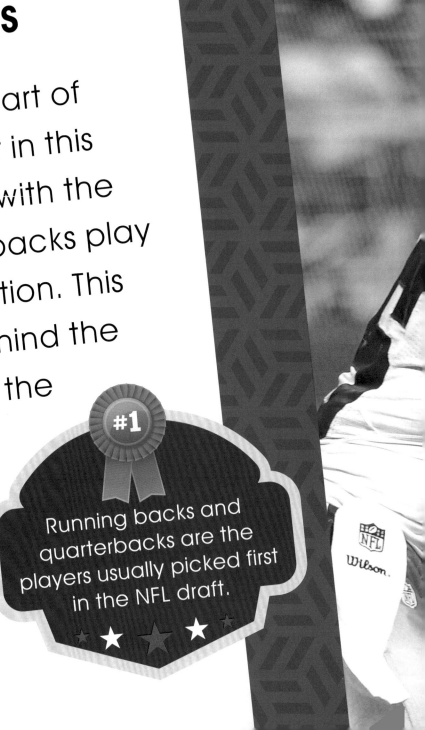

**#1**

Running backs and quarterbacks are the players usually picked first in the NFL draft.

**Jason Witten** is a tight end. The tight end has to block defenders on some plays and catch passes on others. Witten has played with the Cowboys since 2003. He once caught 18 passes in a single game. This is an NFL record. Witten is only the second tight end in history to make more than 1,000 catches.

**Troy Aikman** was the Cowboys' quarterback in the 1990s. He passed the ball 32,942 yards in his career. This is a team record. Aikman won three Super Bowls and was named Most Valuable Player for one of them. He entered the Pro Football Hall of Fame in 2006. He also won the 1997 NFL Man of the Year award.

Famous Player

# Team Records

The Cowboys have won five Super Bowls. Cowboys quarterback Roger Staubach led 23 fourth-quarter comebacks in the 1970s. A comeback happens when a team starts winning only at the end of the game. Emmitt Smith ran with the ball for 18,355 career yards. This is the most of any running back in the NFL.

Emmitt Smith

**18,355**
**Career Yards**

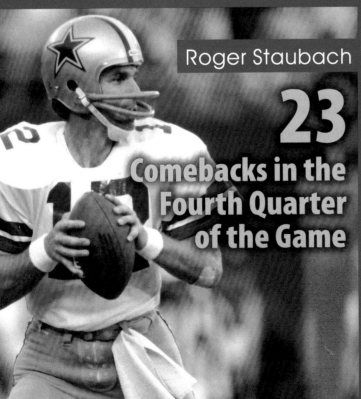

Roger Staubach

**23**
**Comebacks in the**
**Fourth Quarter**
**of the Game**

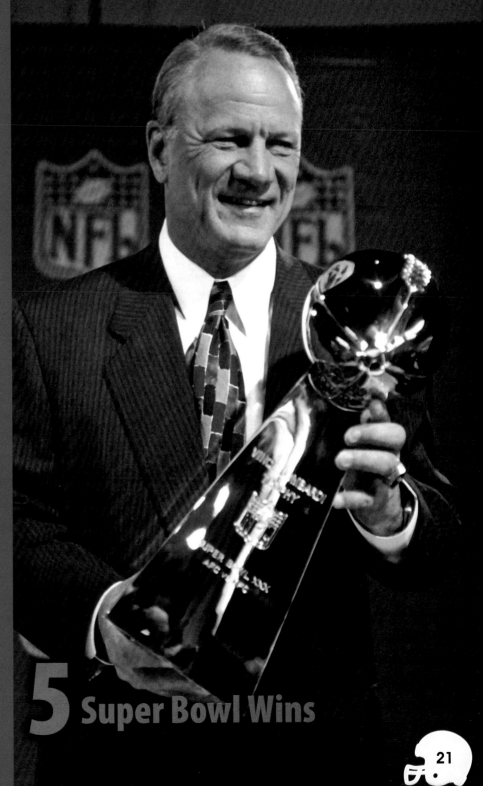

**5 Super Bowl Wins**

21

# By the Numbers

The Cowboys have played in **8 Super Bowls**. Only the New England Patriots have played in more Super Bowls.

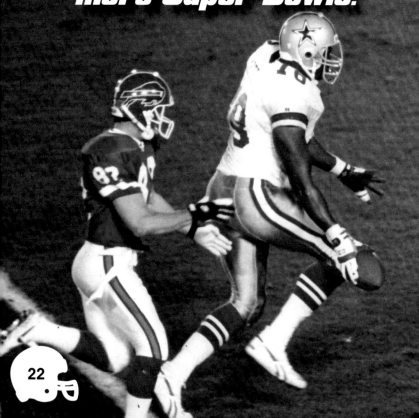

The Cowboys have **sold out** every game **since 2002**.

The team's **first** regular season touchdown was a **76-yard** pass.

The team is worth more than **$4 billion**.

**21** Cowboys are in the Cowboys' own special Ring of Honor.

AT&T Stadium's TV screen is **180 feet** wide.

# Quiz

1. What is the record number of winning seasons the Cowboys had in a row?

2. In what city is AT&T Stadium?

3. Who is the Cowboys' head coach?

4. How many Super Bowls have the Cowboys won?

5. How many yards did Emmitt Smith run the ball in his career?

ANSWERS 1. 20 2. Arlington, Texas 3. Jason Garrett 4. Five 5. 18,355

## Check out www.av2books.com for activities, videos, audio clips, and more!

**1** Go to www.av2books.com.

**2** Enter book code.  D 3 2 2 4 5 8

**3** Fuel your imagination online!

**www.av2books.com**

11-12